THE PINK FACTOR

Julie Marie Myatt

BROADWAY PLAY PUBLISHING INC
224 E 62nd St, NY, NY 10065
www.broadwayplaypub.com
info@broadwayplaypub.com

THE PINK FACTOR
© Copyright 2008 by Julie Marie Myatt

First printing: June 2008
I S B N: 0-88145-377-3

Book design: Marie Donovan
Word processing: Microsoft Word
Typographic controls: Ventura Publisher
Typeface: Palatino
Printed and bound in the U S A

CHARACTERS & SETTING

MARY, *early thirties*
BILL, *early to late thirties*
PEGGY, *early sixties*
CLIFF, *early sixties*
CAROL, *early-mid thirties*
ARTHUR, *mid-thirties*

Time: Present

Place: The Midwest

Maybe pink is not the color of innocence at all, but the first shade of desire. A girl's first glimpse of the beckoning red—the heat and power and excitement of the woman that later comes with that color. Like it or not, the red does come, taking the pink and all that came before with it, as it is washed in a crimson stream down the leg, down the toilet, back down to earth again where it began. But sometimes the red is taken down to darker places, to places it should never have to go, with blunt objects and beasts and screams it never asked to know. The red is dragged to places the pink never could have imagined, nor was it factored in when it was dressed on the new baby girl as she lay in her crib crying for milk, crying for hands to hold her, crying for something better suited for this hungry, dangerous world...

(Slide of a baby girl)

Scene 1

(MARY sits in the audience. She does not address the audience, but looks straight ahead, as if afraid of something behind her.)

MARY: What if, what if you're whole life you've hidden a secret about yourself that you can't get to.... You've locked it away in your body and it's hidden there... deep inside, trapped under a kidney or a lung or a pancreas somewhere, maybe lodged in the marrow of your bones...and you worry it will someday turn to cancer, someday overtake you...or wonder if maybe it already has...

(Lights come up on MARY in the audience. MARY is picking a string from her sexy dress. She looks around. Scared)

MARY: Hello? *(She regains her composure. Checks her face in a compact)* But you're not sure, you see...you're not sure if you have the secret, that kind of disease for certain...only know that because so many girls... *(She stands.)* So very many girls do— *(She adjusts her dress.)* Just because they were made of girl. Because they smelled of morning, fresh apple, peach blossom, chocolate dream faces, dressed with ribbons in their curls, roses in their skin, pink dolls made in their image, tiny tea sets for parties in the afternoon, yellow hats for Easter Sunday, born of sugar and spice and everything nice—

(Slide of a little girl in a dress)

MARY: They were touched. They were fondled, they were grabbed and stabbed in places they shouldn't have been...and you wonder...you can't help but wonder...was I touched too? *(She walks toward the stage.)* Or not? *(She stops and fixes her pantyhose.)* What makes me different? What makes me the same?...Are we all the same?

(Slide of an average looking young white woman.)

(Lights up on a park. Evening)

(MARY walks on stage alone, checks her watch, and continues reading the newspaper, sipping a cup of coffee. She's a stunning sight in her black dress, nice shoes, groomed hair.)

MALE ANNOUNCER: *(O S)* A woman's body was found today in the bushes off Highway 5—

(MARY hears something behind her. She turns to look, sees nothing, and keeps walking.)

(Slide of a simple high-heel)

(Slide of an African-American woman)

FEMALE ANNOUNCER: *(O S)* The search part went home again today with yet another day of disappointment, questions and sadness for the Jones family. Sarah Jones was reported missing Monday—

(Again MARY hears the noise, and stops.)

(MARY quickly turns around a walks faster. Sits on a bench)

(A MOTHER pushing a baby carriage enters and joins her on the bench.)

(Slide of an Asian-American young girl.)

MALE ANNOUNCER: *(O S)* The funeral for five year old Jenny Lee was held today in Walnut Creek—

(MARY *returns to her paper.*)

(*The* MOTHER *takes the baby wrapped in a pink blanket and holds it to her chest.*)

MOTHER: Will it bother you if I...?

MARY: Uh...no..no, go right ahead. How old?

MOTHER: Six months.

MARY: Sweet. (*She returns to the paper.*)

(*Slide of a mother and two daughters*)

MALE ANNOUNCER: (*O S*) The search is over for Margaret Stone and her daughters, Sally and Jessica. Their bodies were found this morning—

(MARY *closes the paper and stares at her cup of coffee before she takes a sip.*)

MOTHER: Big date, huh? (*She rocks the baby. Stands*)

MARY: I'm sorry?

(*The* MOTHER *puts the baby in the carriage.*)

MOTHER: Enjoy it while you can.

(MARY *tosses the paper in the trash.*)

MARY: What?

MOTHER: Get it while you've still got it.

(*The* MOTHER *smiles as she exits with the carriage.* BILL *enters, waving.*)

MARY: But will I ever be able to have that...tiny creatures like that...will anyone ever have a real relationship when maybe their first trust was killed by one hand? One very large callused hand—

BILL: There you are.

(BILL *leans down to kiss* MARY.)

MARY: Oh.

BILL: Bill.

MARY: Bill.

(MARY *awkwardly kisses* BILL *back.*)

(*Slide of* MARY *passionately kissing* BILL *in the dark.*)

BILL: Have you been waiting long?

MARY: No.

BILL: I wasn't sure which end of the park you meant—

MARY: It's just so nice out, I hate to sit in a bar—

(BILL *sits and stretches his arms, surveys* MARY.)

BILL: You look good.

MARY: Do I?

BILL: Yeah. I like that dress.

(*Slide of* BILL *undressing* MARY.)

MARY: Work clothes.

BILL: Where do you work again?

MARY: Bank.

BILL: That's right....right.

MARY: Nice tie.

BILL: Thanks. Tied it myself.

(*Slide of* MARY *undressing* BILL.)

MARY: How are things at the office?

BILL: Dull.

MARY: You haven't worked at a bank.

BILL: At least you give away chairs and toys for opening an account.... You have a big safe. You ever hang out in there?

MARY: Where?

BILL: That safe? Ever sit in there and just stare at all the money?

MARY: No.

BILL: I would. I might even rub my face in it. Get right in the green, you know? Just to fill my nose with all that power. You ever do that?

MARY: No.

BILL: I would. *(He pulls the paper from the trash.)* Yep... All we do is keep selling a false sense of security. *(Combing the paper)* I hate insurance.

MARY: Why do you do it?

BILL: Why do you work at a bank?

(MARY stands.)

MARY: You want to walk?

BILL: No. *(He looks up from the paper.)* I'm comfortable.

(Slide of BILL and MARY in bed)

MARY: What are you staring at?

(BILL places the paper back in the trash.)

BILL: That dress.

(MARY sits down.)

MARY: I'll put it on a hanger and send it home with you.

BILL: I'd rather take it off myself.

MARY: Don't get your hopes up.

BILL: Then why'd you wear it?

MARY: I like it.

BILL: Oh.

(MARY begins to shred the coffee cup.)

BILL: Last time you didn't mind when I—

MARY: I barely know you.

(Slide of BILL *on top of* MARY*)*

BILL: What's to know?

MARY: I don't know. More—

BILL: I'm thirty-seven, I work at a job that means nothing to me but I'm not ambitious enough to go out and look for a new one, I have one fat cat and a loud bird in my one bedroom apartment, mostly decorated by old girl friends, I've never been married, or fathered children, that I know of, I have no idea what I want from my future, other than a nice rider lawn mower and a big enough lawn to use it on, and maybe a chance to play golf once a week.

MARY: Oh.

BILL: What?...

(Slide of MARY *and* BILL *sleeping beside each other.)*

BILL: Without ambition, I'm pretty content with status quo.

MARY: I guess so.

(Slide of MARY *waking up before* BILL*)*

BILL: I don't look for love.

MARY: No.

BILL: Why bother. If you have to look for it.

MARY: Right.

BILL: What's the point.

MARY: What do you look for?

BILL: You enjoyed our last...didn't you?

MARY: I was drunk...actually.

BILL: Were you?

MARY: Yes—

BILL: Let's find a bar.

MARY: I don't want to find a bar.

BILL: Why not?

(Slide of MARY *bringing coffee to bed.* BILL *still sleeping)*

BILL: We had fun.

*(*MARY *has torn the coffee cup to a pile of paper in her hands.)*

(Slide of MARY *sitting in bed, staring out the window.)*

*(*BILL *stands.)*

BILL: Then you're not much fun sober then. Are you.

MARY: Sobering.

BILL: What?

MARY: I could have maggots eating out my heart and earthworms growing inside my cervix...but...drunk and to the naked eye I look—

BILL: You look great.

MARY: I knew a beautiful girl, a very beautiful girl who would try and slash her face about once a year.

BILL: What—

MARY: Her uncle always began be kissing her cheek. She always looked great.

BILL: So?

MARY: And she was a lot of fun in a bar.

BILL: What's that got to do with me?

MARY: Nothing.

(Slide of MARY *looking in the mirror.)*

*(*MARY *crosses her legs, thinking.)*

BILL: Are you coming? Mary.

MARY: What?

BILL: Hurry up.

(BILL *exits.*)

(MARY *stands. She walks across the stage.*)

MARY: When I'm alone I feel it, something, and then I don't want to be alone anymore, I want to be held, with all my clothes on too... If I were found dead we would know, wouldn't we... My ripped apart body a new body of evidence; one massive bloody scar and a wild-eyed frozen scream still pressed on my lips, looking for the nearest ear to whisper— "FIND HIM!". But alive...head still on body. Heart still in chest. Limbs still still reaching—for nothing maybe—but will I know? Who is he, what is his name? (*She stops.*) When did he find me? Where?

(MARY *hears something behind her.*)

MARY: Hello?

Scene 2

(*Slide of* MARY's *empty kitchen.*)

(*Lights come up on* BILL *and* MARY *drunk at a table in a bar.* MARY *has her arm around* BILL:)

MARY: You see...you see Bill, God you smell good... I'm glad I found you because I like you and you know what, I think it's great that you don't ask me any questions. Not one. You really aren't interested in what I have to say or think or who I am really, are you?

BILL: Not directly. No.

MARY: Yes! I love that about you. And your nice stomach muscles and broad shoulders and how your lips feel on my neck—but that's beside the point...I love that you never ask me anything 'cause you know what that's actually perfect because you know, I don't really like to talk about myself much.

BILL: I work out. Sit-ups. It helps.

MARY: See.

BILL: What?

(Slide of MARY's *empty living room.)*

BILL: What?

MARY: I love you.

BILL: What are you talking about?

MARY: Good question. That is a very good question. You know what, I think, I think it may have to do with my—what does it have to do with?

BILL: I don't know—

MARY: Right. Well, I think it may have to do with my family.

BILL: Uh huh.

MARY: No, really, listen. You know why?

BILL: I want another drink.

MARY: My family loves me too much. Too damn much. I don't trust them.

(Slide of Christmas family photo on small table.)

BILL: Drink please?

MARY: So see...if all I do is ask you about yourself and listen to you all night, and believe me, I am only nodding and smiling because I'm pretty good at it by now, and by now, I want really, really want to fuck you later. And you thought I was just being sweet and that your life was that compelling. But you see, it's actually—this arrangement—this you and me and the four, five, six, eighty-seven drinks between us—it's just perfect for me because now I really never have to reveal anything personal about myself now do I?

BILL: I guess not.

MARY: I get to keep all my secrets to myself—

BILL: Where they belong—

MARY: And you feel completely desired at all moments without making one single move, no matter what you're saying or wearing or thinking really—oh, do you think that's where they belong—

BILL: Drink?

(Slide of MARY's *empty bed.)*

MARY: I just don't know about that. Do you like my necklace—

BILL: Sure.

MARY: It was a gift. A token. I'll let you take it off later—

BILL: I'd like to take it off now—

MARY: With your teeth. But. I don't like to rush things.

BILL: No?

MARY: Maybe I should have kept that to myself—

BILL: Everybody thinks they have some damn interesting secrets but most of them are boring as hell.

MARY: What is that cologne you're wearing?

BILL: Safeguard.

MARY: What?

BILL: Soap.

MARY: I like it. Smells fresh. Clean—

BILL: It's soap—

MARY: But secrets you see, but if they're that boring, why are they kept for so long—

BILL: People are idiots—

MARY: Your hair. You should let it go, grow some. Wilder—

BILL: They get confused. They think just because they haven't told anyone something, that it's some deep dark secret, when really, it's just another stupid shit thing waiting for a goddamn ear.

MARY: What if they don't know what it is—

BILL: What? Where the hell is my drink.

MARY: The, the stupid shit thing waiting for a goddamn ear?

BILL: Then they're an idiot. They watch too many television movies or they've read too much fake Freud or some other bullshit like that. You don't forget your own secrets for Christ's sake. That's just stupid. Get a real job or something. Get a hobby. Make a fucking basket. Bake a cake. String glass beads for Christ's sake. Why waste your time on feeling sorry for your sorry ass self...Jesus...you want to go? My drink will evaporate over there before it makes it to the goddamn table.

MARY: What if the basket keeps unraveling?

BILL: Huh?

MARY: The cake tastes like cat shit—

BILL: Let's go back to your place.

MARY: The beads bounce, bounce across the floor—

BILL: Let's go.

MARY: Where?

BILL: Your place.

MARY: Well, it took you long enough.

BILL: What?

MARY: Did you want to talk some more?

BILL: No. Why?

MARY: Thank god. Your lips are begging me for—

BILL: Let's go—

MARY: Well, it's about time.

Scene 3

(MARY's *apartment*)

BILL: *(O S)* What time is it?

(MARY *sits alone in her kitchen, drinking a cup of coffee. Her robe is thrown over her. She's hung-over.*)

(BILL *enters in his boxers.*)

BILL: Hey, what time is it?

MARY: I don't know.

(BILL *pours himself a cup of coffee.*)

BILL: Well, I feel like shit.

MARY: Uh huh.

BILL: Where's your clock?

MARY: In the bedroom.

BILL: You don't have one in your kitchen?

MARY: No.

BILL: That's dumb.

MARY: It's by the bed.

BILL: You should have a clock in here. On the wall or something. Right there maybe. Easy access.

MARY: It's not that far. To walk. Is it?

BILL: Where?

MARY: To the bed.

BILL: I've never walked there. *(He sits across from her at the table.)* So. *(He touches her hand.)* I'm exhausted.

MARY: Yeah.

BILL: Crazy night, huh?

(Slide of MARY's face pressed against her bedroom wall.)

(BILL kisses MARY's cheek. Takes a sip of coffee)

BILL: Good coffee.

MARY: Thanks.

(BILL leans back in his chair.)

BILL: I'm tempted to call in sick.

MARY: Huh.

BILL: Why not. *(He leans in and touches her hair.)*

(MARY stands.)

MARY: I should get in the shower.

BILL: Now?

(MARY pulls her robe together.)

BILL: Can I come?

MARY: No.

BILL: Why not—

MARY: No.

BILL: Why not?

MARY: I want to get clean.

BILL: I'll help you.

MARY: Go home. *(She exits to the bathroom.)*

(The sound of a shower O S)

(BILL takes a sip of coffee. Rubs his face. Scratches his back and discovers it's tender. Looks for blood on his hands)

(Slide of MARY through the shower door.)

(BILL walks over and stands outside the bathroom door.)

BILL: Mary... *(Louder)* MARY.

MARY: *(O S)* What?

BILL: I, I think I'm going to go to work.

MARY: *(O S)* What?

BILL: I GUESS I'LL GO TO WORK NOW.

(Slide of MARY sitting in the corner of the shower)

MARY: *(O S)* O K.

BILL: I had fun last night. Did you?

MARY: *(O S)* Hmm?

BILL: DID YOU HAVE FUN LAST NIGHT? *(He listens.)*

BILL: WHAT?

MARY: *(O S)* SURE.

BILL: Good...I'll call you tonight. Maybe we can get together. *(He listens.)* MARY?

MARY: *(O S)* What?

BILL: I'LL CALL YOU. *(He listens.)* HAVE A GOOD DAY THEN. *(He listens.)* O K? *(He puts his coffee mug on the kitchen table. Touches his back again. Finds a mirror in the apartment and sees scratches on his back.)*

Scene 4

(MARY *packs a suitcase on her bed.*)

(*The telephone rings.*)

(*Slide of* BILL *on the phone with his shoes on his desk.*

BILL: *(O S)* Are you clean?

MARY: What?

BILL: *(O S)* All clean now?

MARY: Who is this?

BILL: *(O S)* Who do you think?

MARY: I don't know...Bill?

BILL: *(O S)* Who'd you think it was?

MARY: I don't know.

BILL: *(O S)* You have a lot of boyfriends?

(*Slide of* MARY *at a bar with a man kissing her neck.*)

MARY: No.

(*Slide of* BILL *doodling while he talks on the phone.*)

BILL: *(O S)* Are you sure?

(*Slide of* MARY *kissing a man in bed*)

MARY: Yes.

(*Same slide of* BILL *with feet on desk*)

BILL: *(O S)* I'll try and believe you.... What are you doing tonight?

MARY: I'm busy.

BILL: *(O S)* Busy with what? One of your boyfriends?

MARY: I'm going out of town.

BILL: *(O S)* Since when?

MARY: Since today.

BILL: *(O S)* Where are you going?

MARY: Home.

BILL: *(O S)* Right. You mentioned that, didn't you?

MARY: No.

BILL: *(O S)* How long you going for?

MARY: I don't know yet.

BILL: *(O S)* Driving or flying?

MARY: Driving—

BILL: *(O S)* So you'll be gone a week? Two weeks?

MARY: I don't know.

BILL: *(O S)* You don't know?

MARY: I'll know when I get there.

(Slide of BILL *sitting stiff behind his desk.)*

BILL: *(O S)* What do you mean?

MARY: I don't know when I'll be back.

BILL: *(O S)* Why?

MARY: I just don't.

BILL: *(O S)* Can I see you when you get back?

MARY: Sure.

BILL: *(O S)* You don't sound sure.

MARY: I am.

BILL: *(O S)* Are you sure?

MARY: We've had two dates—

BILL: *(O S)* And I thought they were good ones—

MARY: Are you looking for something?

BILL: *(O S)* What—no, of course not—

MARY: Then what's it matter if you see me when I get back?

BILL: *(O S)* I like you.

(Slide of BILL closing his eyes in embarrassment.)

MARY: Uh huh. *(She closes the suitcase and sets it on the floor.)* I'll talk to you later.

BILL: *(O S)* Call me when you get back to town. O K? ...Mary?

MARY: We'll see.

BILL: *(O S)* Please?—

(MARY hangs up the phone.)

(Slide of BILL biting his nails, staring at the phone)

(MARY puts on her coat, and grabs her suitcase.)

(Lights fade on MARY.)

(Slides of countryside.)

MARY: *(O S)* Hello.

(Slide of farms)

MARY: *(O S)* Hello?

(Slides of the suburbs)

(Slides of houses. A school)

(Slide of a modest suburban house)

PEGGY: *(O S)* Oh honey, I would have baked something.

Scene 5

(Lights up on MARY's *parents living room. A flowered couch in the middle)*

*(*MARY *and* PEGGY, *her mother, stand in the middle of the room,* MARY's *bags beside her.)*

PEGGY: Why didn't you call?

MARY: It was a last minute—

PEGGY: Still, I barely have enough groceries in the house. Let me run to the store.

MARY: No, Mom, I don't care about that—

PEGGY: No. Sit right there. I'll just run down to store and get some things for dinner. What are you hungry for?

MARY: Nothing—

PEGGY: Chicken? Lasagna? You love my lasagna.

MARY: You don't have to go anywhere. This is why I didn't call. I don't want you to make a fuss—

PEGGY: It's no fuss. Now just grab yourself something to drink and relax. Your father will be so excited to see you.

MARY: Where's Carol?

PEGGY: Oh, I don't know. She's out somewhere. You know how she is.

MARY: Out? Did she move out?

PEGGY: Oh heavens no. You know Carol. She's just "out". And I don't want to know what that means. *(She grabs her purse and coat and runs to the door.)* It's so nice to have you home, dear.

MARY: Thanks—

PEGGY: I still wish you had called. You know how I hate surprises. I don't remember the last time I dusted your room.

MARY: I don't care—

PEGGY: Well, I'll just have to get to it when I get back. Don't you dare go in there. *(She exits.)*

*(*MARY *roams the room.)*

(Slide of MARY *as a girl.)*

*(*CAROL *enters out of breath. She's* MARY's *older sister.)*

CAROL: Hi.

(Slide of CAROL *as a young girl.)*

MARY: Hi...

*(*MARY *walks to hug her.* CAROL *gives a brief hug in return.)*

CAROL: You're home, huh?

MARY: Just for a visit—what's wrong?

CAROL: Nothing.

MARY: Were you running?

CAROL: No. Why?

MARY: You're just...you're out of—

CAROL: I heard you were here. How long you staying?

MARY: I don't know.

CAROL: Yeah.

MARY: You got a hair cut.

CAROL: I hate it.

MARY: Why?

CAROL: I look retarded. You look good.

MARY: You too—

(CAROL *plops on the couch.*)

CAROL: Right.

MARY: Mom went to the store.

CAROL: Yeah, I passed Betty Crocker. Told me not to let you in your room.

MARY: I know.

CAROL: She'll come back with eight bags of groceries, three turkeys, and a ten thousand piece puzzle. Just watch.

MARY: I told her not—

CAROL: Oh, she lives for this. *(She lights a joint.)* Her shining glory.

MARY: What are you doing?

(CAROL *looks at the joint. She takes a deep drag.*)

CAROL: I tell them it's incense.

MARY: They believe it?

CAROL: They can imagine I'm on a spiritual path. Gives them hope.

(MARY *takes the joint and sits down beside* CAROL.)

CAROL: So what are you here for? Money?

MARY: No.

CAROL: Baked goods?

MARY: No. I don't know. I just came home.

CAROL: Why?

MARY: Why not?

CAROL: Why?

MARY: I don't know—

CAROL: What do you want?

MARY: I don't know—

CAROL: Right.

MARY: You stay.

CAROL: Free rent. Can't beat that.

MARY: I thought you were going to live with what's-his-name?

CAROL: Who?

MARY: That guy you were dating—

CAROL: Which one?

MARY: The tall guy with the beard and the eye patch?

CAROL: Who?

MARY: Owned a parrot?

CAROL: A parrot?

MARY: Lived on a boat—

CAROL: Oh. Danny. He was an asshole. Why would I want to live with him?

MARY: You were crazy about him.

CAROL: That pirate shit gets old. Real old. Especially when there's no fucking ocean for a thousand miles.

MARY: You liked him.

CAROL: Tying rope knots around me—

MARY: You were engaged.

CAROL: Only because he made good rum. And I liked his earrings, and he could wear a scarf better than most men. And he did keep a nice clean cabin, but that's it.

MARY: You wouldn't have to live here.

CAROL: And exceed their expectations?

MARY: Who are you dating now?

CAROL: I get at least two square meals a day. Three if I wanted. Laundry services with a smile.

MARY: You have a boyfriend now?

CAROL: What?

MARY: A boyfriend?

CAROL: Oh. Yeah. Guy name Burt. *(She takes a drag from the joint.)* He's kind of dumb, but he's sweet. Calls me his "beauty". I like it.

MARY: Good.

CAROL: Makes up for the million other things that never cross his mind.

(CAROL passes the joint back to MARY.)

CAROL: What about you?

MARY: What?

CAROL: You dating anyone?

MARY: No.

CAROL: Getting laid?

MARY: No.

CAROL: I would think Chicago was good for that.

MARY: What?

CAROL: Getting laid.

MARY: Why?

CAROL: Just seems like that kind of town. All that wind. Blowing people together.

MARY: Not me.

CAROL: Huh.

MARY: Has anyone heard from Arthur?

CAROL: No.

MARY: He doesn't call Mom?

CAROL: Nope.

MARY: Where's Dad?

CAROL: Probably still counting his money.

MARY: The store doing well?

CAROL: How the hell would I know. I don't have a car.

MARY: Right.

CAROL: Is that why you're here?

MARY: Why?

CAROL: You need new tires?

MARY: No.

(MARY passes back the joint.)

Scene 6

(The dinner table. MARY's back is to the audience. She is surrounded by CLIFF, her father, PEGGY and CAROL.)

CLIFF: Nice to have my little Mary home.

PEGGY: Wonderful.

CLIFF: You look like a million bucks.

PEGGY: A little tired, but lovely as always.

CLIFF: A face like that should be married.

PEGGY: Oh yes. Indeed.

CLIFF: Are you dating fools or what?

(Slide of a close-up of MARY's face)

CAROL: How do I look, Dad?

CLIFF: Like a two dollar bill.

CAROL: Really?

CLIFF: You may not add up to much, but there aren't many like you.

CAROL: Thanks, Dad.

CLIFF: No problem, kid.

PEGGY: She just doesn't know her potential.

CAROL: If I did, I could work as a bank teller like Mary.

PEGGY: A bank teller is a fine profession. A service everybody needs.

CAROL: People need my service.

PEGGY: Anyone can work at a drive-through.

CAROL: Mary is a drive-through teller.

PEGGY: Still. She doesn't have to pass out greasy hamburgers and chocolate shakes all day.

CAROL: Somebody's got to do it, Mom. May as well be me.

CLIFF: I like hamburgers. Friendly service at a drive-through can make a big difference in enjoying my ValueMeal. A big difference.

CAROL: Exactly.

CLIFF: Good, friendly, reliable service is the secret to any successful business.

CAROL: We call it the McSecret, Dad.

PEGGY: You could do so much, Carol.

CAROL: But I'm happy with so little, Mom.

CLIFF: That's not a crime.

CAROL: I don't think so.

CLIFF: Appreciate the little things. That's the secret to long life.

CAROL: Smell the roses.

CLIFF: Pet the dog.

CAROL: Drink a case of beer.

CLIFF: Sing in the car.

CAROL: Outrun the police.

CLIFF: Look at your mother.

CAROL: Honk if you're horny—

PEGGY: Who's ready for dessert?

CLIFF: That woman right there can soak more joy out of a bundt cake than a swarm of killer bees.

CAROL: Lives for it.

PEGGY: There's nothing belittling about good homemaking.

CLIFF: No there is not.

PEGGY: I take pride in my work.

CLIFF: That's the secret.

PEGGY: I am not ashamed of my duties.

CLIFF: I wouldn't be where I am without you, sweetie.

PEGGY: And don't you forget it.

CLIFF: How could I? I thrive in your fine work, dear.

CAROL: You are the tire king.

CLIFF: I am.

PEGGY: I'll bring out the pie.

CLIFF: What kind?

PEGGY: Cherry.

CLIFF: Cherry pie. Mary's favorite.

PEGGY: Of course.

CAROL: Cherry pie. That's your favorite, Mary?

CLIFF: Of course it's her favorite. What's his name—

CAROL: Who?

CLIFF: Your brother—

CAROL: Arthur—

CLIFF: Likes pecan. You like apple—

CAROL: I don't like apple—

CLIFF: Of course you do—

CAROL: I hate pie.

CLIFF: You can't hate pie.

CAROL: I do. I'm a cake person. All the way.

CLIFF: Interesting...I just assumed—

CAROL: You were wrong, Dad.

CLIFF: All these years. Does Mary like pie?

CAROL: Of course. But cherry's not her favorite.

CLIFF: It's not?

CAROL: No. It's your favorite.

CLIFF: Mine?

CAROL: Yes.

CLIFF: Oh...hmm...well...don't tell your mother. It'd kill her.

CAROL: Instant migraine.

(PEGGY *enters with a beautiful, huge cherry pie.*)

PEGGY: Look what I have Mary.

CLIFF: Mary's favorite.

CAROL: Get your lips ready.

CLIFF: Now that's a beauty, Peg.

PEGGY: Thank you, honey. You gotta have a lard crust. I don't care what anybody tells you. You gotta have a lard crust.

CLIFF: It's all in the pig fat.

PEGGY: That's the secret.

CLIFF: Send me over a piece of that pig fat. I can't wait to taste it.

PEGGY: Mary's first.

CAROL: Of course.

PEGGY: A nice big piece for our little Mary.

CLIFF: Great to have you home, kid.

PEGGY: It's just wonderful.

CAROL: How long you staying?

Scene 7

(MARY's *childhood bedroom*)

(MARY *sits on the bed. Her suitcase open*)

MARY: Do I have— *(She looks under the bed.)* Where is it? *(She lies on the floor.)* Who was—

CLIFF: *(O S)* Mary? Mary sits up quickly.

MARY: Yes, Dad.

(Slide of CLIFF *holding his reading glasses outside the door.)*

CLIFF: *(O S)* I forgot to tell you something.

MARY: What?

CLIFF: *(O S)* You remember that boy you used to date?

MARY: Which one, Dad?

CLIFF: *(O S)* That tall kid.

MARY: Which one, Dad?

CLIFF: *(O S)* Mack?

MARY: I think so—

CLIFF: *(O S)* He works for me now.

MARY: Really?

CLIFF: *(O S)* Yeah. Good kid. You should come by the store and say hello to him.

MARY: Why?

CLIFF: *(O S)* Well, he speaks highly of you.

MARY: Does he?

CLIFF: *(O S)* That's probably why I hired him.

MARY: Really?

CLIFF: *(O S)* Good kid. Come by and see him.

(Slide of CLIFF *reading the paper.)*

MARY: I'll try.

CLIFF: *(O S)* Oh...and there was another man...Paul. Do you remember Paul?

MARY: Not really, Dad.

CLIFF: *(O S)* He said he went to elementary school with you.

MARY: Huh.

CLIFF: *(O S)* He came in a couple weeks ago. Nice kid. Bought some all season radials.

MARY: Great.

CLIFF: *(O S)* He said to tell you hello.

MARY: Thanks, Dad.

CLIFF: *(O S)* His brother...what was his name...Alan. Alan said to say hello too.

MARY: Thanks, Dad.

CLIFF: *(O S)* Seems like all the boys still love you.

MARY: Oh yeah?

CLIFF: *(O S)* I love you too, kid.

MARY: Thanks, Dad.

Scene 8

(Slides of breakfast foods. Pancakes. Eggs. Bacon. Boxes of cereal)

MARY: *(O S)* I'm not hungry.

PEGGY: *(O S)* What do you mean you're not hungry?

MARY: *(O S)* I'm not hungry. I've got things to do.

PEGGY: *(O S)* What kind of things? I thought you came home to visit.

(Lights up on MARY at the table. PEGGY above her)

MARY: I did.

PEGGY: Then where are you going?

MARY: I'm just going out.

PEGGY: I don't know what you girls do with yourselves. "Out" there. It makes me worry.

MARY: Don't worry.

PEGGY: I'm a mother. If you girls would ever have children of your own—

MARY: Maybe we won't.

PEGGY: What?

MARY: Have children of our own.

PEGGY: Don't say that.

MARY: It's true.

PEGGY: You only say it to hurt me.

MARY: It's the truth.

PEGGY: You girls like to torture me. I spend my whole life doing all I can to give you the best, and more I might add...I never got a thing from my mother, not one thing, and you and your sister both say things like that to hurt me. I'll never understand it.

MARY: You should have had sons.

PEGGY: You're right. I should have. They appreciate a good meal. They don't go on diets four times a year and slam their doors in my face every time I want to sit down and have a heart to heart talk.

MARY: Mom, you had a son.

PEGGY: He doesn't count.

MARY: Why not?

PEGGY: He was just like you girls. Too big for his britches. Ungrateful. I packed his lunch for sixteen years and he never took it to school.

MARY: You should have stopped packing it.

PEGGY: What kind of mother would do that?

MARY: The kind that takes a hint.

PEGGY: If I took every hint that came my way from this family, Mary, I would shrivel up and die from disappointment, now wouldn't I? A woman can only take so much.

MARY: You're right.

PEGGY: If you're going to devote yourself to raising three beautiful kids right and keeping a husband fed and satisfied and a household neat, clean and tidy, you have to keep your nose in the Pine Sol and your head in the oven as far as I'm concerned.

MARY: Bye, Mom.

PEGGY: But, let me tell you, little girl, I know this house inside and out and if you think you and your sister and your brother have ever kept any news, hints or secrets from me, you've got another think coming. I know my kids like the back of my hand.

MARY: You think so?

PEGGY: I know so. Clothes don't lie, Mary. I may have washed, dried, folded and put them away for you like any good mother would, but I saw it first, didn't I? All of it. All your antics. The beer. The smoke. The grass—and I'm not talking about that marijuana—I don't want to know about that—I saw the river mud. The car grease. The hay and the barn dust. The basement couches. I could track you kids like a well-trained poodle just by going through the hamper.

MARY: Then tell it to me. *(She stands.)*

PEGGY: What?

MARY: My secrets. All of them. From the ground up.

PEGGY: Don't mock me, Mary. I don't appreciate that. You had clean clothes every day of your life.

MARY: I'm not mocking you. I'm asking you. I want to know.

PEGGY: Asking me what?

MARY: Where'd it all start?

PEGGY: You girls speak in tongues sometimes—

MARY: Who was he?

PEGGY: Who?

MARY: The one who started it?

PEGGY: I'm not a mind reader, Mary. I'm your mother—

MARY: Who was he?

PEGGY: Who? Have some juice or something, will you—

MARY: Do you know who he was?

PEGGY: Who who was?

MARY: Him?

PEGGY: Him? God? He's above, Mary—

MARY: No—

PEGGY: Who? Santa Claus? The tooth fairy? Easter Bunny? I've told you all about them already.

MARY: A man. I'm asking you—

PEGGY: A man?

MARY: Yes! No! Maybe. I don't know.

PEGGY: Well...gosh, Mary. There were so many, I mean—

MARY: I know, but the first—

PEGGY: Mothers used to call me daily to tell me how their boys had fallen for you—

MARY: Mom—

PEGGY: I tried, but couldn't hide my pride, I mean—

MARY: Mom, not them—

PEGGY: I did make those dresses. I did comb your hair and tie those bows. My pink and precious Mary. Who could resist you—

MARY: Mom! Was there someone else?

PEGGY: Who?

MARY: In my room maybe—

PEGGY: Well...gosh...that's a tough one—

MARY: I know but please.

PEGGY: There was a man you thought lived in your closet for awhile—

MARY: What?

PEGGY: But I put a chair against it and you outgrew him after a few months and eventually just fell asleep if that's who you mean—

MARY: I don't know—

PEGGY: And you did imagine one of your stuffed rabbits—Roger I think you called him—had fleas and made me bathe him. Three times.

MARY: Really?

PEGGY: Yes. Then you made up something about a short man living between the walls of your sister's room and yours and whistling through his nose at night.

MARY: Oh?

PEGGY: But that wasn't long after we took you to see Snow White and you were seeing little men everywhere. You made the dog move out of his dog house just to make room.

MARY: What if it was true?

PEGGY: Mary, if I believed everything you and your sister ever told me I would be a pretty stupid lady, now wouldn't I? You know how many times you told me their cars broke down? The teacher kept you late? His mother made cookies so you had to stay for them to cool?

MARY: That did happen.

PEGGY: Kids would rather burn themselves to high heaven.

MARY: I didn't always lie.

PEGGY: No. You did not. You were a very sweet, honest, good little girl. Everyone said so. I swear, walking around town with you, was like walking with my own little Shirley Temple.

MARY: What happened?

PEGGY: Your sister got a hold of you.

MARY: What happened to her?

PEGGY: Arthur stepped in.

MARY: What happened to him?

PEGGY: Oh, he was born that way. I'm sure of it.

MARY: How?

PEGGY: He was born breech, Mary. It's a scientific fact. He left his real good brains in my womb.

(MARY *walks away.*)

PEGGY: Mary—you didn't eat a thing—where are you going?

MARY: Out.

Scene 9

(*Lights come up on* MARY *by a watering hole, throwing stones.*)

(*Slide of a river*)

MARY: What if you were meant to be a fish and then it wouldn't matter who did what to you or what you did to whom...Your tail would just be one among many, swimming. It wouldn't matter if you had secrets; the sea was full of them but none of them mattered. They were all washed away by the water. Drowned by land—

CAROL: Mary! *(She runs on stage in her McDonald's uniform. Out of breath.)* What are you doing?

MARY: Why—

CAROL: Did you follow me?

MARY: No. Why?

CAROL: Are you on your way out?

MARY: No.

CAROL: Oh. Have you seen Burt?

MARY: I don't think so—

CAROL: I only get half an hour.

MARY: So why come here?

CAROL: I'm asking you.

MARY: I'm just looking.

CAROL: For what? That top drawer of things you left in the bushes?

(Slide of MARY's now neat drawer of folded underwear.)

CAROL: With the action this spot gets, there's probably enough panties in these shrubs to outfit a small tribe in New Hampshire or something.

MARY: Still?

CAROL: Hell. I think half this town was conceived here. The other half were aborted before they made it to the christening. Damn that Burt. I gotta start pinning things to his shirt. Mind like a sieve.

MARY: How often you meet out here?

CAROL: Two, three times a day.

MARY: Why don't you meet at his place?

CAROL: He lives in his car. Damn it. I ran all the way down here for nothing.

MARY: You ran here?

CAROL: Yeah.

MARY: Across town, under the highway, through the Robert's field and over?

CAROL: Yeah.

MARY: Damn.

CAROL: You used to do it.

MARY: No—

CAROL: Yes—

MARY: Maybe in high school we'd drive but—

CAROL: Six years old you started coming here.

MARY: No...

CAROL: Yes.

MARY: Did Arthur show us?

CAROL: No way. He started partying out of town when he was ten. You found this place on your own.

MARY: I did?

CAROL: Showed it to me.

MARY: No.

CAROL: Yes!

MARY: I did?

(*Slide of small shoes on grass*)

CAROL: In the summer we'd put on flip flops and walk down here. Take them off on the way. Then came the Carlson boys.

(MARY *casts a stone.*)

CAROL: All those damn sun dresses Mom made for you that got torn. If you had eaten as much as I did, you wouldn't have to wear them, you know. You could have worn shorts and a halter.

MARY: They weren't so bad—

CAROL: That yellow one with the apples on it you liked—

(*Slide of balloons*)

MARY: They were balloons.

CAROL: Whatever. It ripped down the back and you cried all the way home. I had to give you my whole weeks allowance to shut you up.

MARY: It worked?

CAROL: It was five bucks. Those Carlson boys were something. Couldn't catch you though.

MARY: What were we doing?

CAROL: Damn that Burt.

MARY: What were we playing?

CAROL: You were there.

MARY: I know but—

CAROL: God, Mary. Hide and seek or red light green light. Maybe T V tag. Something stupid like that.

MARY: Did we get a lot of mosquito bites?

CAROL: What?

MARY: I have these scars on my legs. Holes.

CAROL: You scratched too hard.

MARY: They itched.

CAROL: So? Scratching never stopped them from itching, did it? It just made them bleed.

MARY: It made me feel better.

(Slide of blood on her legs.)

CAROL: So now you have scars. Dummy.

MARY: Why would we play where there were so many mosquitoes anyway?

CAROL: We didn't care. Jesus. Besides, the Carlson's cousin came to town that one summer and that was it. Taught us a new game.

MARY: What color hair did he have?

CAROL: I don't know.

MARY: Brown?

CAROL: No. He's a Carlson. They all have red hair.

MARY: White skin.

CAROL: Pink really.

MARY: Right.

CAROL: Slap, kiss and hug.

MARY: What?

CAROL: That was the game.

MARY: Who?

CAROL: Now that kid was fucked up.

MARY: What did he do?

CAROL: But he was all talk. *(She checks her watch.)* Damn it. I gotta go back to work. Listen, if you see Burt, tell him I'm pissed.

MARY: O K.

CAROL: What a waste. Hey, come say good-bye before you leave. *(She starts to walk away.)*

MARY: Why doesn't he just pick you up?

CAROL: There's not enough room in his stupid car.
(She exits.)

*(*MARY *casts another stone. Looks down at her legs. Scratches)*

MARY: "You sit behind the person and they guess what sign you've given and if they get it right, you get a kiss. If they get it wrong, you get a slap. If they think you're giving no sign and they get it right, you get a hug. You go first, Mary."

(Slide of a convenience store)

(Slide of a tire store)

(Slide of school parking lot)

(Slide of a school)

(Fields)

Scene 10

(Slide of junk yard)

(Slide of various cars)

(Slide of the inside of an old car)

*(*MARY *sits holding a steering wheel.)*

MARY: Who was he?

(Slide of clothes on the floor of a car)

(Slide of MARY *in the back seat with a man)*

(Slide of her shoes against the window.)

(Slide of the car on the road.)

(Slide of MARY *smiling in the passenger side.)*

(Slide of A different young man beside her.)

(Slide of the countryside)

(Slide of a barn.)

Scene 11

(Slide of the wreckage of the inside of a barn.)

*(*MARY *wanders on stage, picks up an empty liquor bottle. She walks up to an old rack, looks at it. Picks up a shovel. Puts it down)*

(There is a tarp covering something in the corner.)

(A porn magazine hangs out from the edge. MARY *picks it up and looks at it. Tosses it aside. She lifts up the tarp to look for more, and a little shoe falls out. Stands staring. She reaches in and pulls out the body of a naked broken doll with its head popped off. The legs and arms tumble to the ground. The head. A little pink dress. She picks up the pieces of the doll. She puts the head back on. The arms. The legs. She throws the dress aside. Stands staring at the doll)*

(Slide of McDonalds sign)

Scene 12

*(*MARY *enters with the doll behind her back as* CAROL *stands smoking.)*

*(*CAROL *stands smoking a cigarette in her uniform.* MARY *enters.)*

CAROL: What? You coming to say good-bye?

MARY: Did I like that guy?

CAROL: What guy?

MARY: The Carlson's cousin.

CAROL: What?

MARY: Did I like him?

CAROL: Like him?

MARY: Yeah.

CAROL: I don't know. No.

MARY: He was skinny wasn't he. Freckles.

CAROL: Of course. He's a red head.

MARY: Pimples?

CAROL: You wouldn't let him near you.

MARY: What about the game?

CAROL: You wouldn't play.

MARY: Never?

CAROL: Not that I saw.

MARY: How about you?

CAROL: Of course. I was the only girl. *(She adjusts her visor.)*

MARY: You think we were touched? *(She drops the doll.)*

CAROL: That's kind of a stupid look for you.

MARY: What?

CAROL: Carrying a naked doll. Where's her dress?

MARY: Were we touched?

CAROL: What?

MARY: Were we touched? As girls.

CAROL: This is only a fifteen minute break.

MARY: Were we touched?

CAROL: What do you mean?

MARY: As little girls. Do you think something happened to us?

(Slide of blurred photos)

CAROL: Like what?

MARY: Like we were abused.

CAROL: By who?

MARY: I don't know. That's why I'm asking.

CAROL: No.

MARY: How do you know?

CAROL: I think I'd remember something like that. So would you.

MARY: Girls block it out.

CAROL: Not me.

MARY: Maybe I did.

(Slide of blurred image)

CAROL: No you didn't. Don't be stupid.

MARY: Are you sure?

CAROL: Yes.

MARY: Then what's wrong with me?

CAROL: I don't know.

MARY: Why are we so fucked up?

CAROL: Speak for yourself.

MARY: I do!

CAROL: What, you think Dad or Arthur or someone came into your room or my room and played under our panties or something?

MARY: I don't know—

CAROL: Please.

MARY: I don't know. It's possible—

CAROL: Not in our house it isn't.

MARY: If a man, I don't know who, got a hold of me, when I was little, and messed me up, and I forgot it, tried to forget it and it's stuck—

CAROL: Maybe you messed you up. Ever think of that?

MARY: Yes, but—

CAROL: Maybe you were born that way.

MARY: What way?

CAROL: Not everybody's born a good little girl. No matter how many cute dresses their mother makes for them and makes them wear. While the mother's other daughter could have been wearing horse hooves for all she cared—

MARY: I know, but—

CAROL: So you've fucked around. Played in the bushes. Made out in cars. Bumped it up in barns. So what?

MARY: But why?

CAROL: It makes you feel good.

MARY: No it doesn't.

CAROL: You're lying

MARY: It doesn't anymore.

(Slide of MARY's *drunk face)*

CAROL: Then don't do it.

MARY: I can't. That's the problem. And I don't know where it comes from—

CAROL: Well, I don't know what to tell you. If that's what you're here for. You weren't "touched" or fondled or abused or molested or whatever you want to call it by anyone I know. I can't help you. And it's kind of a stupid question if you ask me.

MARY: Why?

CAROL: It just is. It would kill Dad if you asked him that. If he knew you thought that. He still thinks you shit ice cream. And Arthur? Arthur never cared enough about us to talk to us, much less touch us. So you're unhappy so you come home. You can't find the right guy to love you, you're not getting enough attention, you need Mom and Dad to pat your pretty head, blah, blah, blah. Boo hoo. You want to blame someone for fucking every guy you see because you can, and, you enjoy it. You only feel guilty about it because you think you should because Mom and Dad stuck you with a stupid name like Mary.

MARY: There's more to it than that—

CAROL: What?

MARY: I think there's a secret I can't—

CAROL: What? What could it be?

MARY: I don't know—

CAROL: What would you do with it anyway?

MARY: I don't know—

CAROL: Find a place to point your stupid finger? It wouldn't change anything—

MARY: It might. I've looked everywhere—

CAROL: Well you're not going to find it here. In our house. Mom has cleaned every inch of that place so there's nothing dirty in it now. Believe me—

MARY: But I can't listen to the news or read the paper anymore 'cause I'm afraid I'm going to be next somehow because maybe I'm going to do something or wear something I shouldn't have one day just because I knew it would make men look at me because I like the way that feels, I love it, actually, when the man I want notices me, desires me, I feel so powerful and free for that moment...

(Slide of a dead woman)

MARY: But if it's the wrong kind of look, from the wrong guy who thinks I want his attention, I could be in the gutter down the road, locked in the trunk of a car, in the barn, or floating down the river with the rest of the fish—

CAROL: All I know is if there's dirt in your panties, it's your own. You made it. You don't see me pointing any fingers—

MARY: Face down, lipstick still perfect, arms out, still soft with lavender lotion—

CAROL: You have everything, Mary. You always have. You're just too stupid or afraid to enjoy it. So you like sex. Big deal. At least you've got your own apartment to do it in. *(She exits.)*

(Slide of tire store)

Scene 13

(Tire store. CLIFF sits on a tire with a cup of coffee.)

(MARY enters. CLIFF stands.)

CLIFF: There she is!

MARY: Hi Dad.

CLIFF: What are you up to? Carol called and said you stopped by. Combing your old stomping grounds, huh?

MARY: Something like that.

CLIFF: Coffee?

MARY: No thanks.

CLIFF: Well, we've got what you call a Slow Day.

MARY: Looks like it. Where is everyone?

CLIFF: Lunch.

(MARY *sits on a tire.* CLIFF *sits opposite.*)

CLIFF: You just missed them.

MARY: Who?

CLIFF: The boys. They just went to lunch. I'm holding down the fort, so to speak.

MARY: Looks good, Dad. It's really shiny in here.

CLIFF: Oh yeah. Of course. I believe in a clean business. That's my secret. These babies have plenty of time to get dirty once they leave, but in here, I want the customer to smell nothing but rubber and the possibility of a smooth ride.

MARY: It smells like rubber alright.

CLIFF: I love it, kid. I gotta say. I love that smell. And, if I may brag, all this rubber did pay your way through community college.

MARY: Yes. It did.

CLIFF: I always thought you'd go further. But.

MARY: Me too, Dad. Dad?—

CLIFF: If you're happy, I'm happy. Right? So how's it going there in the big city?

MARY: Oh. Fine. But Dad—

(*Slide of* MARY *laughing and flirting with a man*)

CLIFF: Good. Glad to here it. You make me proud, kid.

MARY: I do?

(*Slide of* MARY's *face pressed against the wall with* BILL.)

CLIFF: Branching off on your own like that. Braving the big world by yourself. Away from home. Hell, look at Carol. She only knows the thirty mile radius of our house and her job and whatever else is there in between. And frankly, kid, with her, I don't want to know what's in between. But that, that makes a father think, kid, it really does...a man wants to think he raised his daughters to take care of themselves and look, with her, I may have failed. But with you, my job as a father, has been a success.

MARY: You think so?

(Slide of MARY *in the shower, crying)*

CLIFF: I know so.

MARY: What about Arthur?

CLIFF: There was never any hope for him. If he could have had Harley Davidson stamped on his Pampers, he would have. Yep, I bought him his first Big Wheel, and that was the beginning of the end.

MARY: Why?

CLIFF: That kid wanted freedom. Nothing a father can do with that really but buy him a good helmet and step out of the way.... But you, Mary. There was always something different, something special about you.

MARY: What?

CLIFF: I can't explain it. Like, like you Mary, were already twenty-one when you were only two.

MARY: Oh?

CLIFF: And when you were a teenager. Thirty-seven. I remember that first dance you went to in high school. What do they call it that again—

MARY: Prom?

CLIFF: Right. The Prom Dance. And you walked out of your room in that long dark blue dress and I swear it was like a stranger walked out. Like we put you in that little pink nursery with all those mobiles and toys we bought for you or took from Carol, and then you came out fifteen minutes later but it was actually fifteen years later and you were a young woman. I didn't know what happened. I didn't know where my little girl went. I didn't know what to do—

MARY: Mom made that dress for me. Strapless with a bow in the back—

CLIFF: And so I cried. I just sat down in my easy chair and put my face in my paws and cried and your mother couldn't understand what on God's earth was wrong with me and I couldn't explain it to her really so she kept bringing me beer. And more beer.

MARY: I had some beer that night myself, I think—

(Slide of the dress beside a car)

CLIFF: And it scared me, kid. That kind of thing scares a father. That beauty. And that he helped produce it. Somehow. And I know I'm no, no Robert Redford and so that makes it's even more remarkable. But there you were.... And then I stated thinking about the men. I'm a man and I know men, kid. I've been around them all my life. I hear them. I see them. You want your little girl to be safe, you know?

MARY: I know. But—

CLIFF: Hell, I think I would have kept you in here if I could.

MARY: In here?

CLIFF: There's a lot of rubber in here, kid. A lot of rubber.

MARY: There is.

CLIFF: What else can the tire king give his girl?

MARY: I don't know—

CLIFF: How are yours holding up?

MARY: What?

CLIFF: On that car of yours? The tires. You rotating them?

MARY: Oh. Yes, Dad. They're fine.

CLIFF: An even tire is a safe tire.

MARY: Right.

CLIFF: Rain, shine or snow. A good radial could save your life, kid. That's the service I provide.

MARY: You do it well, Dad.

CLIFF: Thanks, kid. A man needs to hear that now and then. Huge profits and an expanding inventory aren't enough sometimes. Hell, what am I telling you that for. You work at a bank!

MARY: I do.

CLIFF: Money gets old, doesn't it?

MARY: Yes, Dad.

CLIFF: Yep. Thank goodness for family. Now that's something to sink your teeth into. Love. And I'm not talking about sex. You know I'm not all for talking about that kind of stuff. It does make me uncomfortable to hear that kind of talk. I am a Christian man at heart and I don't like that kind of talk. It makes it cheap and dirty. If you ask me. But love. Mary, that is something to sink yourself into. You just wait.

MARY: How long do I have to wait?

CLIFF: Pardon?

MARY: I'm waiting.

CLIFF: You're going to steal someone's heart yet. You just wait 'til these boys get back. They think you are the bees knees, you know that?

MARY: Really?

CLIFF: Absolutely. You see that stack of tires over there?

MARY: Uh huh.

CLIFF: If that were a pedestal, you'd been on top.

MARY: That's up to the ceiling, Dad.

CLIFF: You might have to bend your head down a bit.

MARY: Right.

CLIFF: But that's up there, isn't it?

MARY: It looks pretty wobbly.

CLIFF: Rubber, kid. Safety's angel. Besides, I'd always be here to catch you if you fell.

Scene 14

(MARY's *childhood bedroom*)

(MARY's *under the bed, grabbing things.*)

(*Slide of* PEGGY *looking through the keyhole.*)

(*The doll sits on her bed, next to her bag. She grabs items from around the room. Her pillow. Old clothes. A photo album*)

PEGGY: (O S) We don't want to eat without you.

MARY: You do it every day, Mom.

PEGGY: (O S) Don't you think we want a break from that for goodness sake? What are you here for if you're not going to spend time with us?

MARY: I don't know.

PEGGY: (O S) Then come down to the table. It's getting cold.

MARY: Go ahead.

(*Slide of* PEGGY *trying to pick the lock.*)

PEGGY: (*O S*) Why'd you lock the door? You girls always lock the door like you think there's going to be bandits running through the house or something.

MARY: Because I don't want you to come in.

PEGGY: (*O S*) Well, you've got a whole apartment to yourself in Chicago that I never come into now don't you? You could ask me to visit now and then. We could go shopping or something fun like that. Have lunch together—

MARY: Your dinner's getting cold.

PEGGY: (*O S*) What are you doing in there?

MARY: Nothing.

PEGGY: (*O S*) Can't you do that in Chicago?

MARY: No.

PEGGY: (*O S*) Well, I don't want you doing it here either. I've spent all day stuffing a turkey for you and I'm not going to have you sit up here doing nothing while we sit down there and try and enjoy ourselves. Now. Unlock this door.

(MARY *finishes packing her bag.*)

PEGGY:(*O S*) Mary?

(MARY *checks under the bed again.*)

PEGGY:(*O S*) Mary—you girls are so darn secretive. You'd think I was a Russian spy.

(MARY *carries it to the door and unlocks it.*)

PEGGY: The table's all set—what? You just got here—

MARY: I never said I could stay.

PEGGY: Then why come? If you're just going to turn around and leave. This isn't just your come and get it quaint little bed and breakfast, Mary.

MARY: I'm know, but—

PEGGY: Cliff?! She's leaving!

CLIFF: *(O S)* What?

PEGGY: Mary wants to leave!

(CLIFF *enters with a glass of scotch and the paper.*)

CLIFF: What's the matter?

PEGGY: She says she's going back.

CLIFF: When?

PEGGY: Now.

CLIFF: Why?

PEGGY: How would I know. No one ever tells me anything. May as well be a lizard they way I'm kept in the dark.

(CAROL *enters drinking a McDonald's milkshake.*)

CAROL: Leaving, huh?

PEGGY: She thinks we're a B and B.

CAROL: Well, nice having you.

CLIFF: Stay another night—

PEGGY: Please, Mary. We've barely seen you—

CAROL: Let's not pressure her.

PEGGY: It's not much to ask.

CLIFF: Really. Your mother's made the last supper down there and we need some help taking some pounds off that turkey.

CAROL: Mary's had turkey before—

CLIFF: Have you seen that thing, Carol? That bird is the size of a Lincoln. Stuffed to the gills.

PEGGY: Stuffed, basted and roasted all day. Just for tonight.

CLIFF: Looks delicious, Peg.

PEGGY: Thank you, dear. I do try.

CAROL: What's the big deal. It's not Thanksgiving.

PEGGY: Everyday is Thanksgiving as far as I am concerned when my family is happy together—

CLIFF: Bounty. Hands that runneth over. Now that's something to celebrate. Makes a man proud, girls. That's what I have to offer—

(Slide of blurred childhood photo)

MARY: Do you have Arthur's address?

CLIFF: What?

MARY: Arthur's address.

CAROL: Why?

MARY: Mom?

PEGGY: Oh, there's been so many, Mary. He's made a mess of my address book. What do you need that for?

CLIFF: He wants to be left alone. He's made that very clear.

PEGGY: It seems we've never really been good enough for him.

CLIFF: Tattooed enough is more like it. I gave him a top-notch Gillette razor for Christmas one year and he used it to shave his head. What are you gonna do with a kid like that? Walking around looking like Mister Clean.

CAROL: Give him a hat.

CLIFF: I gave him a hat the next year and he cut the top out of it and wore it like a collar. I washed my hands of him.

PEGGY: You don't want his address, Mary. You don't want to see him really now do you?

MARY: Why not?

PEGGY: I think you just need another night of rest in your old cozy bed, with those stars on the ceiling, see, I left them all there for you, and a good meal in your little belly—

CAROL: Arthur's got nothing for you, Mary.

PEGGY: I don't even think he's got heat at his place much less a bathroom—

MARY: I want to see him.

CAROL: Why?

MARY: He's my brother.

CAROL: So.

CLIFF: He's my son, but that doesn't mean I want see him. Some things are just kept better out of sight, out of mind, Mary. You learn that as you get older. Some things just aren't worth the effort.

CAROL: Amen, Dad.

PEGGY: Oh but you can still love him.

CLIFF: Of course.

PEGGY: From afar.

CLIFF: Three towns over is far enough.

PEGGY: He really never did bathe enough, Mary.

CLIFF: He stunk.

PEGGY: I don't know where he got that.

CLIFF: Hell, Peg. You can lead your kids to water, but you can't make them bathe now, can you?

PEGGY: It was much easier when I could put them all in a tub together.

CLIFF: Three ducks in a row—

CAROL: Where nothing happened.

PEGGY: Just scrub you all at once.

CAROL: Everyone's hands in the water. Away from each other.

PEGGY: Oh, you kids had your hands on everything. You'd think I was washing the Helen Keller trio.

(Slide of blurred bathtub)

CAROL: But not on each other.

PEGGY: The fists. God help me. I should have been paid to referee. Mary's lucky to be alive after some of your beatings, Carol. You were a cruel girl. I'm sure Mary's still got scars from your fingernails clawing at her every five minutes. I had her checked for rabies several times.

CAROL: Sisters.

MARY: Arthur's address please?

CAROL: Skip it, Mary.

MARY: Why?

CAROL: He's innocent—

CLIFF: What? No. I think he's still got another year on probation. Right, Peg?

PEGGY: I lose track.

CLIFF: And he can't leave the state.

CAROL: Mary can.

CLIFF: Sure she can. She knows how to work in a bank, not rob it.

PEGGY: Oh Mary. What is your hurry, honey? There's a boyfriend calling your back, isn't there—

CLIFF: That's our little girl. She's always been in a hurry—

PEGGY: You girls drop me like a hot ham when a boy is involved—

CLIFF: Looking for something, rushing to find it. She didn't crawl long, did she, Peg?

PEGGY: Oh no. She went straight to walking.

CLIFF: Then running. I guess you're just a go getter, kid.

CAROL: Then let her go get it—

PEGGY: It does hurt my feelings. The boys may come and go, but a mother's love will never leave you, Mary. Remember that. Remember that next time you slam the door in my face. Lock the door. I have feelings too. Big ones. I did make you, didn't I?

CLIFF: Twenty hours of labor.

PEGGY: Thirty, dear.

CLIFF: But worth every minute of it.

PEGGY: Of course. She was perfect. She made the Gerber baby look like a ferret.

CAROL: How was I, Dad?

CLIFF: Like a prize circus peanut.

PEGGY: She came out a month early, pink and shriveled, then took two weeks to let out a cry.

CLIFF: Been squawking ever since.

PEGGY: People kept asking if we were going to raise you ourselves.

CAROL: Don't we have a turkey to eat?

CLIFF: Both of them were criers.

PEGGY: They were.

CLIFF: And what's his name.

PEGGY: It was all we could do to sleep through it.

(Slide of blurred image of crib)

CLIFF: We wore ear plugs for six years.

PEGGY: But they learned.

CLIFF: We were not at their beck and call.

PEGGY: But always here to love them.

CLIFF: Of course.

PEGGY: Of course.

CAROL: Turkey?

CLIFF: I am hungry.

CAROL: Let's eat.

CLIFF: I'm always hungry.

CAROL: A family trait.

CLIFF: Big appetites.

CAROL: Born with it.

PEGGY: Well, if there's something good and tasty on the table, of course you're going to eat it.

CLIFF: You've spoiled us, Peg.

PEGGY: I suppose I have spoiled all of you. It's my fault. I can't help myself, I aim to please.

CLIFF: Not a crime.

MARY: Arthur's—

CAROL: Drive safe, Mary. We'll be thinking of you. Call if you can.

PEGGY: But leaving so soon, Mary. It's really not fair. We were so excited and I worked so hard to make everything so absolutely perfect for you—

CLIFF: Oh, c'mon. No tears. She'll be back. Right kid?

MARY: Sure. But—

CAROL: Don't rush. You know it's just boring old us here. Twiddling our thumbs.

CLIFF: They usually come back for something.

PEGGY: Not near often enough.

CLIFF: Some stay forever and other's never come back and some we just can't hold. Right, kid?

Scene 15

(*Slides of trailer homes*)

(MARY *stands waiting. A torn out page of the telephone book*)

(ARTHUR *enters, a plunger in his hand.*)

ARTHUR: Well now. Who's this?

MARY: Hi Arthur—

(ARTHUR *shakes her hand, then hugs* MARY.)

ARTHUR: What are you doing here?

MARY: I didn't want to barge in on you.

ARTHUR: Hell, you could have barged. I'm a barger from way back.

MARY: It's been so long—

ARTHUR: You look great.

MARY: Thanks. You too.

ARTHUR: And I don't even try.

MARY: You manage the whole place, huh?

ARTHUR: Yeah. It's about forty units.

MARY: Forty—

ARTHUR: Which means about eighty toilets.

MARY: Keeps you busy?

ARTHUR: Busy enough. What are you doing here?

MARY: I just went home for a bit. Thought I'd see you on my way back—

ARTHUR: What a surprise.

MARY: Yeah.

ARTHUR: What were you doing home?

MARY: Visiting.

ARTHUR: How are they?

MARY: Same.

ARTHUR: Same.

MARY: Yeah.

ARTHUR: Hell. It works for them.

MARY: And you?

ARTHUR: What?

MARY: Everything going well?

ARTHUR: Sure. You know. Same.

MARY: Right.

ARTHUR: You want a beer or something?

MARY: No.

ARTHUR: I have a six pack in the fridge, we can sit and—

MARY: I can't stay long. I just wanted to see you.

ARTHUR: Alright.

MARY: Say hello.

(*They stand in an awkward silence.*)

ARTHUR: Hello.

MARY: Hi.

ARTHUR: You sure you don't want a beer—

MARY: No. I just wanted to see what you were up to.

(*Slide of his old room. Heavy metal posters. Bongs*)

ARTHUR: Nothing much—

MARY: Ask you a question.

ARTHUR: Ask away.

MARY: Did you ever touch me?

(*Another awkward silence*)

ARTHUR: Hit you?

MARY: I know you hit me.

ARTHUR: Right—

MARY: I mean touch me.

(ARTHUR *puts down the plunger. Stares at* MARY)

ARTHUR: No.

MARY: I know it's an awful question, Arthur, but—

ARTHUR: You asked it.

MARY: I did...

ARTHUR: You did.

MARY: I'm sorry but—

ARTHUR: Never.

MARY: Any of your friends—

ARTHUR: No.

MARY: Are you sure?

ARTHUR: They'd be dead.

MARY: Are you sure—

(ARTHUR *picks up the plunger.*)

ARTHUR: Anything else?

MARY: No. I, I guess not—

ARTHUR: Nice to see you.

MARY: Yeah. You too.

ARTHUR: Take care of yourself.

MARY: Sure. You too—

ARTHUR: Call next time. (*He exits.*)

(MARY *watches him go, then slowly exits in the opposite direction.*)

Scene 16

(*Slide of fields*)

(MARY *walks through the slides.*)

(*A rest stop*)

(*She stops.*)

(*A bill board stops her. It's full of posters of missing women. Warnings about the rest stop.* MARY *quickly exits.*)

(*Slides of urbanity*)

(*She looks around.*)

Scene 17

(Slide of MARY's *apartment. Her bedroom)*

*(*MARY *spreads the stuff from her suitcase on the bed. Smells it. Looks through the photo album)*

(Slides of the blurred images on the wall continue. Every image is overexposed or underexposed images of MARY. *Pink hazy blurs.)*

(She closes the album. She places the doll on the bed. Touches its face)

(Slides of MARY's *empty kitchen. Empty living room.)*

*(*MARY *sees a pair of high heels in the corner.)*

Scene 18

(Slide of a bar)

*(*MARY *stands outside, looking around, deciding whether to go in.)*

(A WOMAN *enters, heading for the bar.)*

WOMAN: Looking for something?

MARY: Pardon?

WOMAN: Are you looking for something?

MARY: I don't know—

WOMAN: Happy hour ends at six.

MARY: Oh—

WOMAN: Lady's Night starts at eight. *(She exits.)*

MARY: Thanks.

(Music begins.)

(Slides of bottles of booze)

(Men smoking in the bar)

(Men staring straight at the camera)

(MARY stands looking around, a beer in hand.)

(Slides change of various angles of men staring.)

(MARY begins to move to the music. A sexy, slow dance)

(She continues to move as the slides of the men change.)

MARY: And then what if you discover that after all, you're nothing more than just a pretty girl who needs a lot of attention...because without it you may not exist...what if your secret is nothing more than you asking to be touched...over and over again...by whom ever would reach for you...

(Slide of four hands oddly pressed against a wall.)

Scene 19

(MARY's apartment)

(BILL and MARY lie in bed.)

BILL: I missed you.

(MARY tries to sleep.)

(BILL reaches over. He pulls something from under the pillow.)

BILL: I really missed you. *(He rubs it against her back.)*

(MARY sits up.)

BILL: You sleep with her? *(He turns the dolls legs and arms, turns the head until it pops off.)*

(MARY takes it from him, grabs the head.)

BILL: You get that at home?

MARY: I found it.

BILL: What are you going to do with it?

MARY: I don't know.

BILL: It's gross.

MARY: What?

BILL: It's dirty.

MARY: I'll wash it. *(She puts the head back on.)*

BILL: Wash me instead.

MARY: No.

BILL: Who knows what's on me after last night—

MARY: I'd rather not.

BILL: Why not?

MARY: I'm not interested.

BILL: I can change your mind.

MARY: No.

BILL: C'mon. Bathe me.

MARY: No—

BILL: I have a nice body.

MARY: So bathe yourself.

BILL: Then let me bathe you. *(He reaches for her.)*

*(*MARY *pulls away. Stands up)*

BILL: Where are you going?

*(*MARY *puts on her robe.)*

MARY: To sit in the tub.

BILL: Let me come.

*(*BILL *stands up and walks over to* MARY.*)*

MARY: No.

BILL: Why not?

MARY: I don't want you to.

BILL: What's with you?

MARY: Nothing. *(She walks away.)*

BILL: You like me or not?

MARY: What?

BILL: Do you like me?

MARY: Not really.

(BILL grabs MARY.)

BILL: Why do you keep calling?

(MARY shrugs.)

(BILL shakes MARY.)

BILL: Why do you call?

(MARY shrugs.)

BILL: Why do you call me?

MARY: Because you'll come.

(MARY plays with the doll. BILL grabs the doll out of her hands and throws it across the stage.)

BILL: I want you to like me.

MARY: Why?

(BILL pushes her against a wall.)

BILL: What's wrong with you?

MARY: Nothing.

BILL: I want you to like me.

MARY: I'm sorry.

BILL: What's wrong with you?

MARY: I don't know.

BILL: What are you hiding from me? (*He spreads her legs with his foot. Pull her hair.*) Give it to me.

MARY: What?

BILL: I want it.

MARY: What?

BILL: Give it to me.

MARY: I, I can't.

BILL: I want you.

MARY: I'm sorry.

BILL: I want you. (*He pushes himself up against her.*) I want you to like me. When you're not drunk.

MARY: But—

BILL: Like me.

MARY: I'm sorry.

BILL: Love me.

MARY: I'm sorry.

(BILL *pulls her to the ground.*)

BILL: What's wrong with you? Why can't you love me?

MARY: I don't want to.

(BILL *takes a bottle from the floor and breaks it. Puts the glass to* MARY's *throat.*)

BILL: Can't you love me? (*He is on top of her.*) Love me.

MARY: Why?

(BILL *holds* MARY's *arms up with one hand, the glass in the other.*)

BILL: What's wrong with you?

MARY: I don't know.

BILL: Tell me what's wrong—

MARY: Nothing.

BILL: Why do you call me?

MARY: You come.

BILL: Why can't you love me?

MARY: I'm sorry.

BILL: What's wrong with me?

MARY: Nothing.

BILL: Tell me. *(He runs the glass down her chest.)* Who is he?

MARY: Who?

BILL: Him.

MARY: Who?

BILL: Him. The one you love.

MARY: There's no one—

BILL: Who is he?!

MARY: I'm not sure—

BILL: Tell me.

MARY: I, I think he's bigger than you.

BILL: How?

MARY: I don't know.

BILL: Tall?

MARY: Huge.

(BILL kisses MARY's breast, while his hand holds the glass beside it.)

BILL: And?

MARY: He's reckless.

BILL: Mean?

MARY: No. Fearless.

BILL: How?

MARY: He won't leave me alone.

BILL: Who is he?

MARY: I don't know—

BILL: Where'd you meet him?

MARY: I didn't meet him. He—

BILL: What?

MARY: Found me.

BILL: Where did he find you?

MARY: I don't know.

BILL: Think!

MARY: I am.

BILL: Where were you?

MARY: I'd been in the woods maybe.

BILL: The woods—

MARY: Rolled in some leaves.

BILL: He found you in the woods.

MARY: No. Not there—

BILL: Where?

MARY: Well—

BILL: Where?

MARY: When I came home, my mother put me in the tub. She left me there alone. She had to finish dinner—

BILL: When?

MARY: I don't know—

BILL: When? *(He pushes the robe aside with the glass.)*

(Slide of leaves floating on water)

MARY: I sat there, watching the small pieces of leaves beginning to float up on the water. I reached for the soap. It fell in the water.

BILL: Where was he—

MARY: Between my legs.

BILL: When—

MARY: I was seven.

BILL: Seven—

MARY: I reached for it again. Brushed against myself. I stayed there. Forgot the soap. I stayed there. My hand free in the water. I found myself. And I didn't want to let go. I stayed there.

(BILL lets go of MARY's arms and thrusts his hand between her legs.)

BILL: Here?

MARY: My mother walked in. And slapped my hand. My mother found the soap.

(Slide of soap floating on water.

MARY: And scrubbed me clean. Scrubbed me.

(Slide of blood mixing with water; a rose hue)

MARY: She put me in my white nightgown with the roses she stitched on the collar. And sent me to bed. She told me I was catching something. I needed to sleep before it got serious.

BILL: And?

MARY: When she turned off the light.

(Slide of a window in the dark)

MARY: I held up my hand. I saw it's shadow on the wall. Made a bird with my fingers. A bird with strange feathers. The bird's mouth moved—

(BILL's mouth moves down MARY's body.)

BILL: Where was he—

MARY: It became a hawk.

(Slide of dolls left on a shelf in the dark)

MARY: All I could see was him. All I could feel was him.

(Slide of tiny shoes by the bed in the dark)

MARY: The hawk cried through the night. He was hungry. He was wild—

BILL: Mary—

(Slide of tiny dresses hanging in the closet in the dark)

MARY: He was lonely.

BILL: Mary—

(MARY moves and is on top of BILL. The glass in her hand)

MARY: His tongue was wet.

BILL: I love you.

MARY: His claws ripped inside my tiny chest—

BILL: I love you—

MARY: He was still hungry.

Scene 20

(BILL *kneels alone on the stage in a towel. His hair is wet. He's picking up pieces of glass.*)

(MARY *enters the stage wet. She is wrapped in a towel and carries the doll, now clean.*)

BILL: Be careful—

(MARY *steps around* BILL.)

BILL: Funny what a little water will do, huh?

MARY: Uh huh.

BILL: Just wakes you up. Ready for the day. Those soap commercials really don't lie.

MARY: Yeah.

BILL: It's like "Wow" some days, you know?

MARY: Uh huh.

BILL: Like "Zing! I'm clean. Let's go new day!"

MARY: Uh huh.

BILL: I tried not to use all the hot water. Did you have hot water?

MARY: Yeah.

BILL: Maybe that's not a problem in your building.

MARY: No.

BILL: It's a big problem in mine. I take more cold showers than is natural.

MARY: Did you find your clothes?

BILL: They say a bath actually uses less water than a shower. Did you know that?

MARY: Yes.

BILL: Hard to believe, isn't it? *(He stands with the glass in his hands, searching a place to put it.)* Seems like a lot of water. Especially if it's a big tub.

MARY: I thought you were going to get dressed— *(She steps on a piece of glass.)*

(She hobbles to the bed.)

BILL: Are you O K?

MARY: Goddamn it.

BILL: Are you bleeding? *(He stands over her, the glass filling both his hands.)* Is it bad?

MARY: No.

BILL: Let me see. *(He takes a closer look.)* Oh yeah. It must be in there deep.

MARY: It's not bad—

BILL: You never can tell. You gotta get it out. It'll get infected.

MARY: It's fine. Really, just—

BILL: No. Really. It happened to me once.

MARY: It's fine.

BILL: You can't leave it in there.

MARY: I can handle it. You go ahead and get dressed—

BILL: Do you have some tweezers or something? I can remove it for you.

MARY: No.

BILL: C'mon—

MARY: I'll do it myself.

BILL: No, please. Let me help.

MARY: I can get it out myself.

BILL: I won't hurt you. *(He walks around, looking for a place to dump the glass in his hands. He finally finds his clothes on the floor and dumps the glass on top.)* Do you have a first-aid kit?

MARY: No.

BILL: You don't keep a first-aid kit in your apartment?

MARY: No.

BILL: Why not?

MARY: I don't know. I don't think about it.

BILL: But what if you get hurt?

MARY: I just—

BILL: I know what I'm going to buy you first. *(He exits into the bathroom.)* But don't worry. I'll find something. We'll get it out. And I promise.

(MARY sits holding her foot.)

BILL: I won't hurt you.

(MARY sees the doll beside her. She picks it up and her hand covers it with blood. She places it against her chest.)

Scene 21

(Slides of women in sexy dresses, feeling free walking down a busy sidewalk.)

(A woman walking through a park.)

(MARY sits in the back of the audience in a red dress in the dark.)

MARY: So what if your secret will change nothing?
...Your best dress your best target? Another girl floating

down the river...face up? Lips still pink and pursed for a kiss?

(Slides end on a woman's mouth—it's unsure if it's a mouth of pleasure or fear.)

MARY: Hello?

END OF PLAY